L BAY PRESENTS

THE STUDENT VIOLINIST'S BOOK OF ROUNDS

BY
MARILYN
WORTH

Visit us on the Web at http://www.melbay.com — E-mail us at email@melbay.com

Dedicated to:

Leila Blackburn Worth

&

George Granville Worth

Who taught me early in life that children,

and the activities of childhood are very much worth one's time and energy.

FOREWORD TO THE STUDENT

This is a collection of rounds and canons that spans a period of some eight centuries. It is a rich and varied collection of music that celebrates life and is great fun to play.

The round, sometimes called a catch, is a form of "counterpoint" music. Everyone plays the same melody. Harmony is produced when each musician staggers their entry into the song. The result is often times quite beautiful. Rounds are the music of friends, the music of equal companions.

"SUMER IS ICUMEN IN," one of the rounds in this collection, is noteworthy in that it is the earliest recorded round. It was scribed on parchment by John of Fornsete, a monk at Reading Abbey, England—scribed sometime between 1226 and 1240. It is not known who in fact wrote the piece, probably not John of Fornsete. Most of the early rounds were written anonymously. But, as time went on, as music developed, the most prolific composers of rounds were also the great composers of the day.

By the 17th century, the round as a musical form reached its heyday, especially in England. It was England's Golden Age of music, and the round was its most popular form of a song. For both King and commoner, it was the custom of the time to gather after dinner for the singing of rounds.

I find it very interesting that during this same period of time, from the 13th to the 17th century, England was developing a new social idea called democracy.

In 1215, the Magna Carta was signed, which allowed "free men" to control some of the abuses of those in power. By the 17th century, parliamentary government was a reality—a weak reality perhaps, but fact no less—and France and the American colonists looked on with interest.

The influence that music has on us can be profound. I have no doubt that rounds as a form (equal part music) both instructed and supported this democratic ideal wanting to be born out of the human psyche. And, as the ideal of equality needs to be reborn again in each of us, perhaps rounds as a form can still instruct us. At the very least, they can provide musicians with a great deal of musical pleasure.

As a young person, as most of you are, you will have less interest in ideas about music and more interest in playing music, and this is how it should be.

This collection is my attempt to start you off with the most enjoyable music possible. I want you to experience as quickly as possible—in full—the pleasures of making music, and to encourage you to hold on to it for a lifetime.

NOTE TO THE TEACHER

My beginning strings orchestra is a "round" orchestra. I find that rounds make the best "first" orchestra music for young students.

— Everyone gets to play the melody. Viola, cello and bass players are equally challenged.

— Sections of the orchestra can be balanced according to head count, not instrumentation.

— The fugue form tightens up the musical intellect and helps students develop an autonomous rhythmic sense like nothing else can.

— And, you do not need a room with a piano for rehearsals.

The great majority of these pieces were written as music, to please as music. They are the products of the musical mind, not the pedagogical mind, and as a result they satisfy the authentic musician that lives within even the youngest of students.

I put my name on this collection as the selector and editor. Unfair! The list of contributors should also include the names of at least ten years of students. This is a student choice collection of pieces, and as a result this collection meets the needs of students better than anything else I have ever used.

PLEASE NOTE:

Tradition tells us to repeat a round song for as many times as there are voices. Thus, a three-part round would be repeated three times; a four-part round would be repeated four times, etc.

Please note the use of fermatas. Most rounds end as they begin, with each voice dropping off as it finishes out the song. But with some rounds, all voices end together. The fermata simply indicates the end of the piece for a part.

TABLE OF CONTENTS

FRESHMAN LEVEL REPERTOIRE

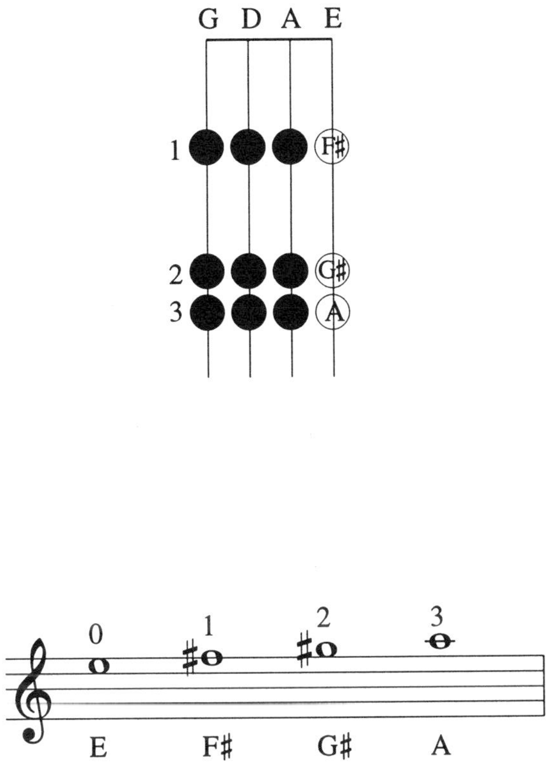
G D A E
1 F♯
2 G♯
3 A
0 1 2 3
E F♯ G♯ A

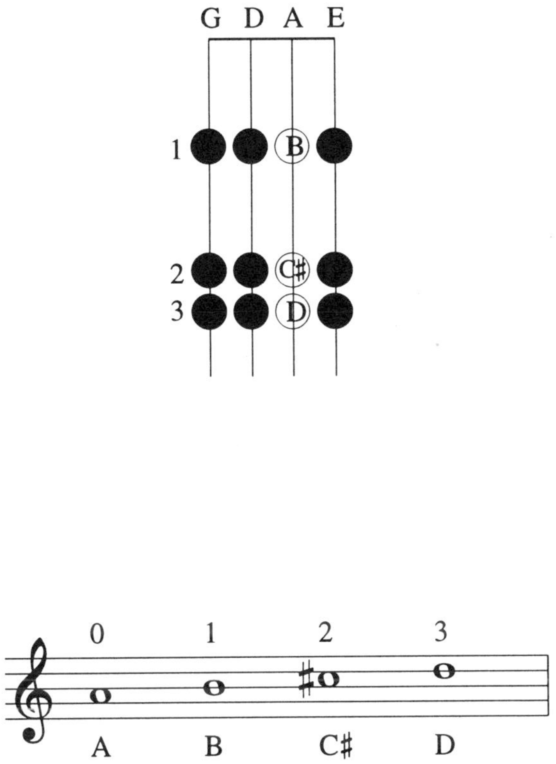
G D A E
1 B
2 C♯
3 D
0 1 2 3
A B C♯ D

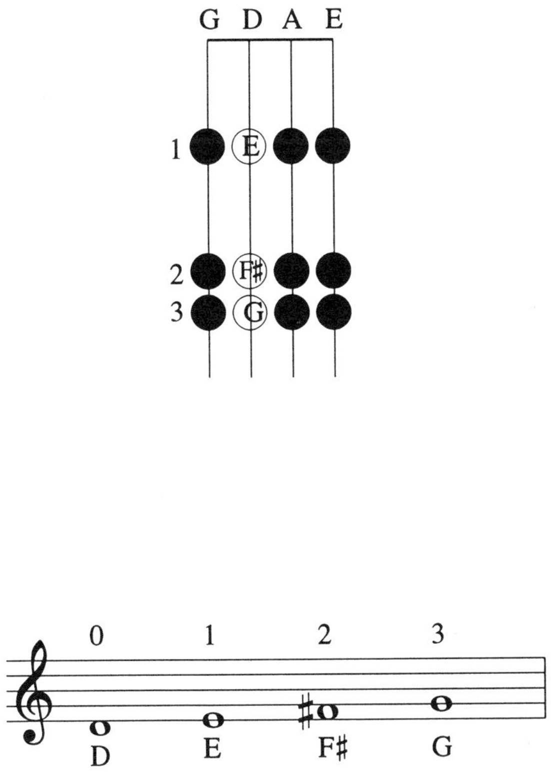
G D A E
1 E
2 F♯
3 G
0 1 2 3
D E F♯ G

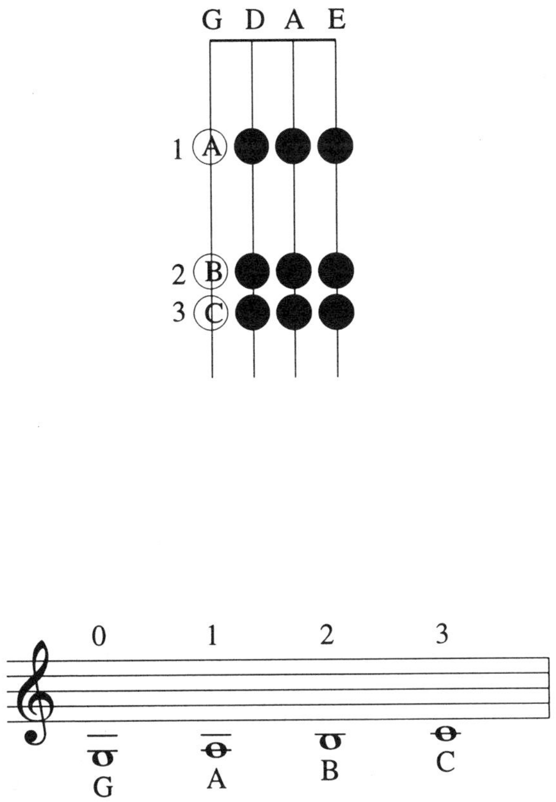
G D A E
1 A
2 B
3 C
0 1 2 3
G A B C

ADRIAN'S SONG

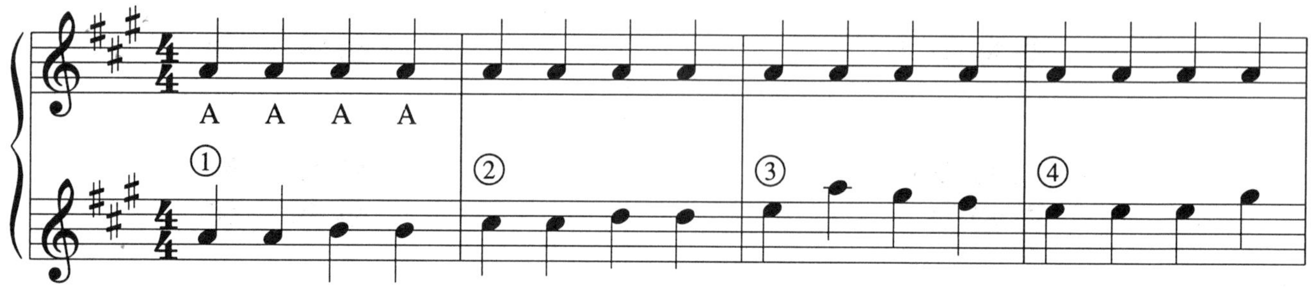

Orchestra Part

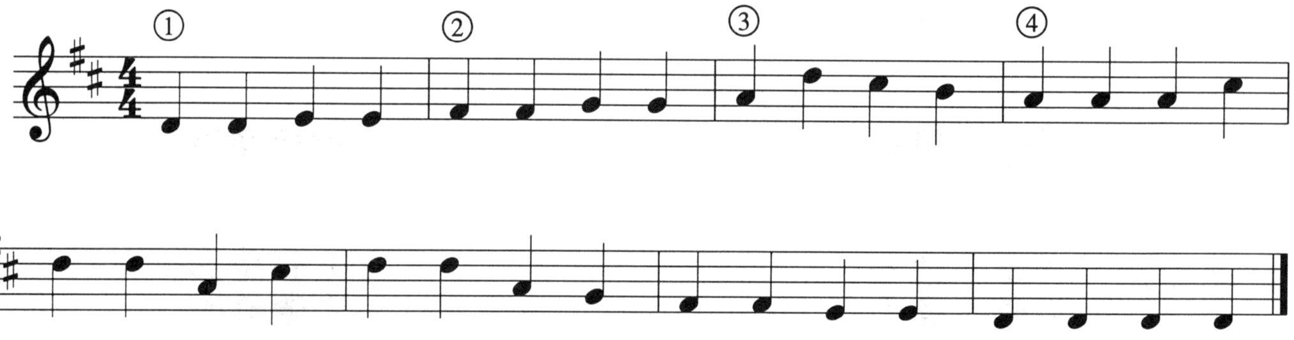

EDWARD'S SONG

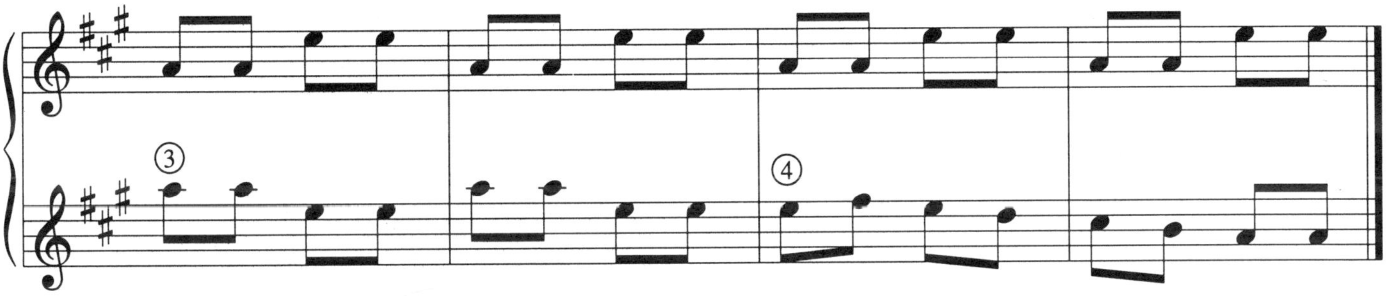

Orchestra Part

SCOTLAND'S BURNING

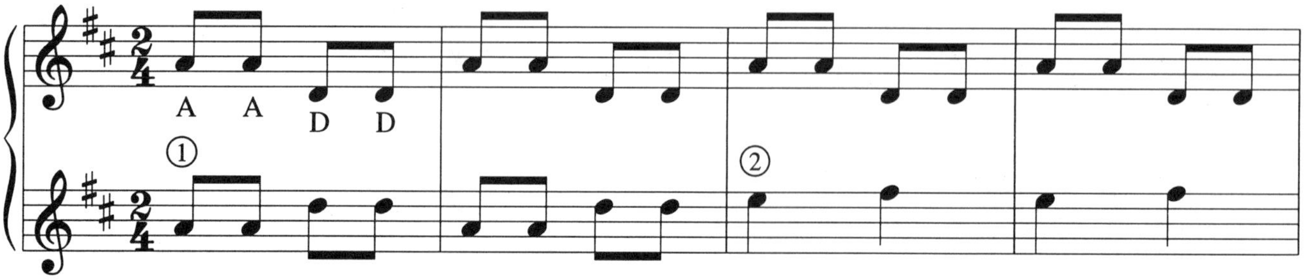

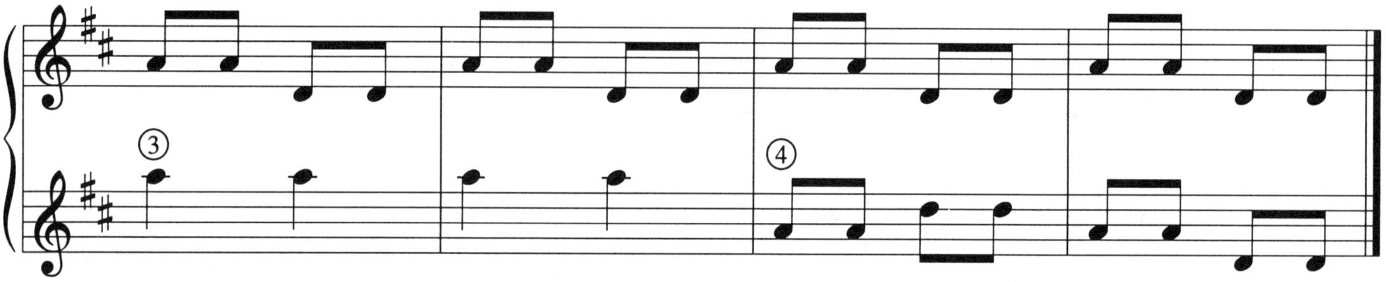

Orchestra Part

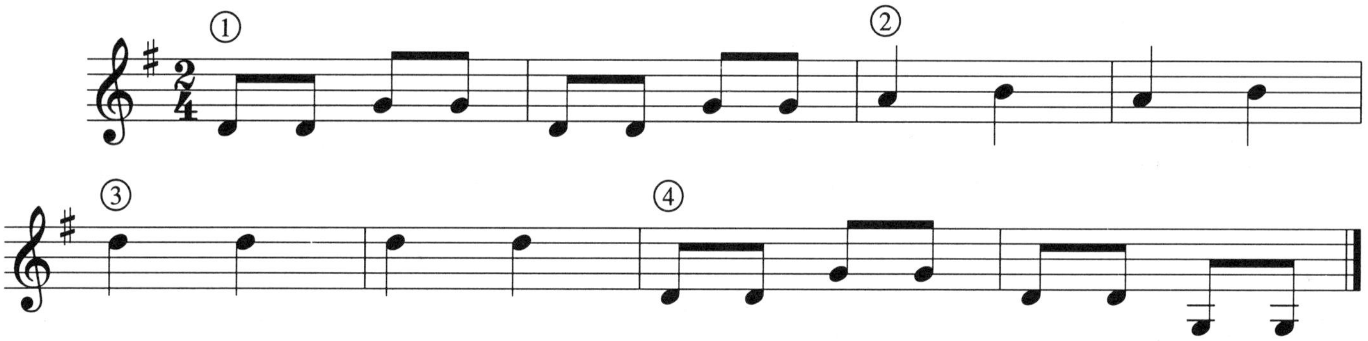

Danish

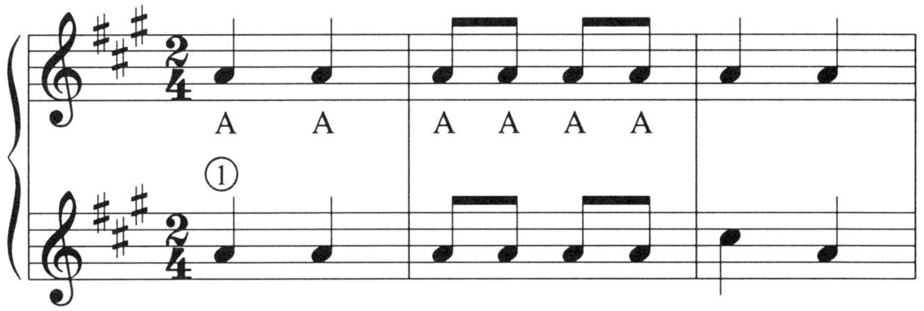

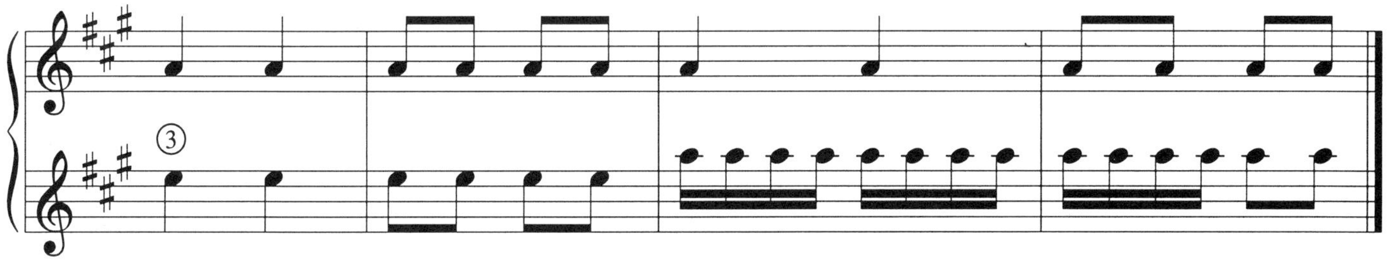

Orchestra Part

ROWBOAT

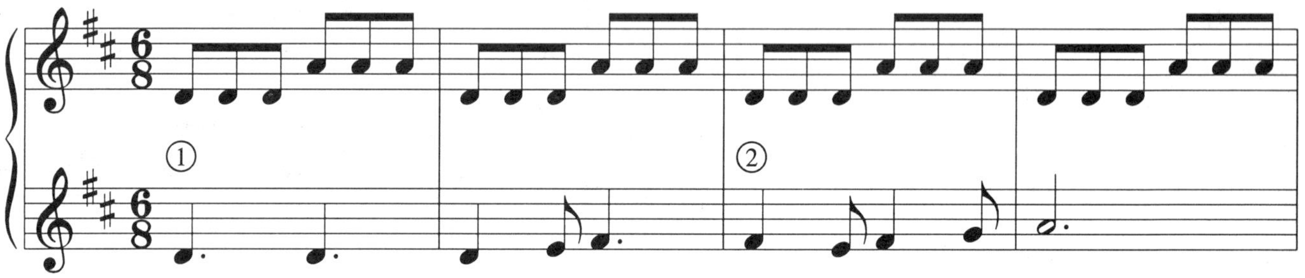

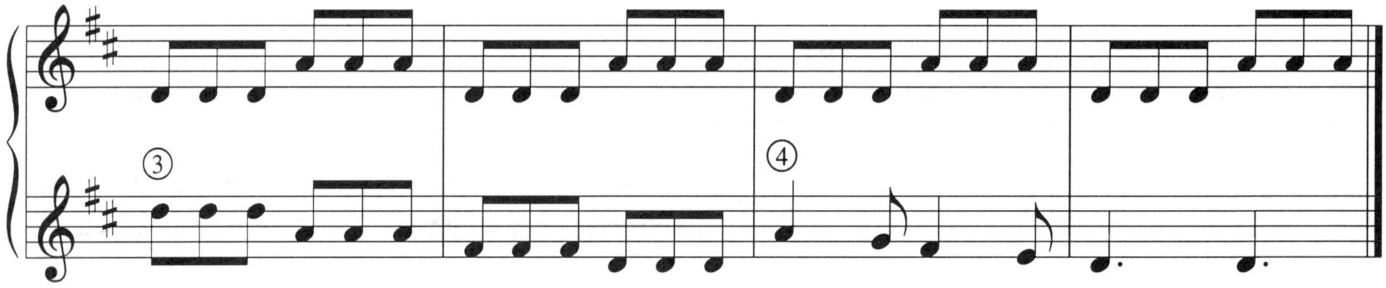

SONS OF THE SEA

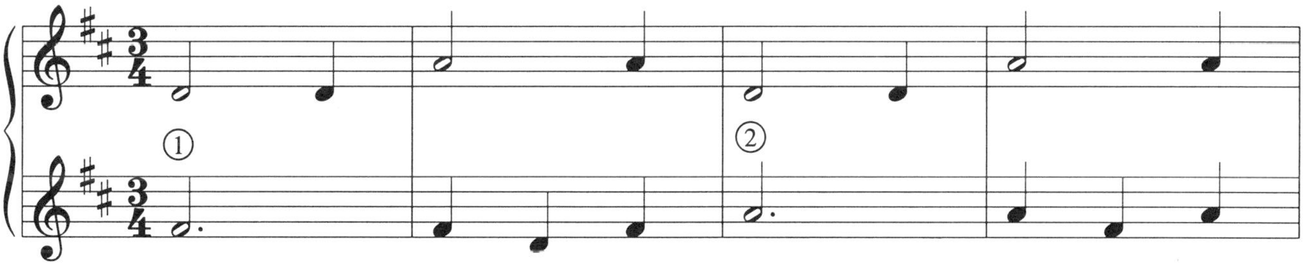

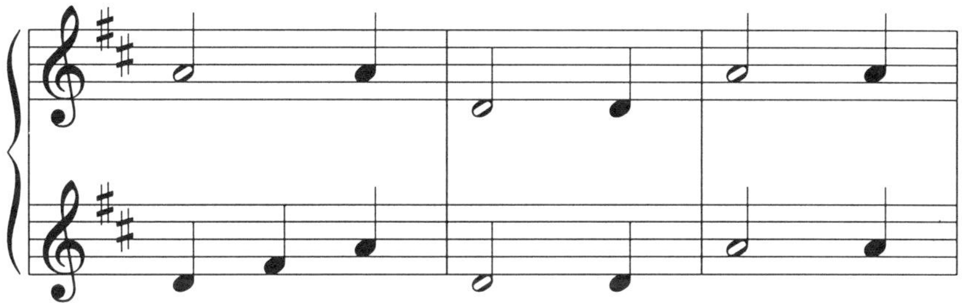

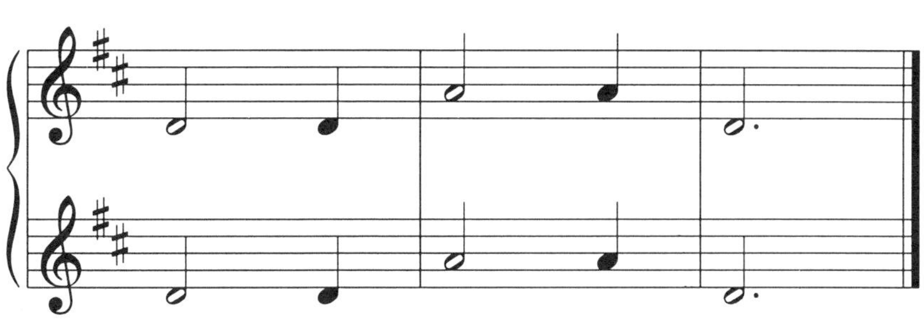

COME AGAIN, HO

English

Orchestra Part * See page 32

NEARLY DONE

ALLELUJAH, AMEN

DEAR FRIEND

VIENNESE MUSICAL CLOCKS

Zoltan Kodaly

SHAKER LIFE

Shaker Round
Elder Issachar Bates 1835

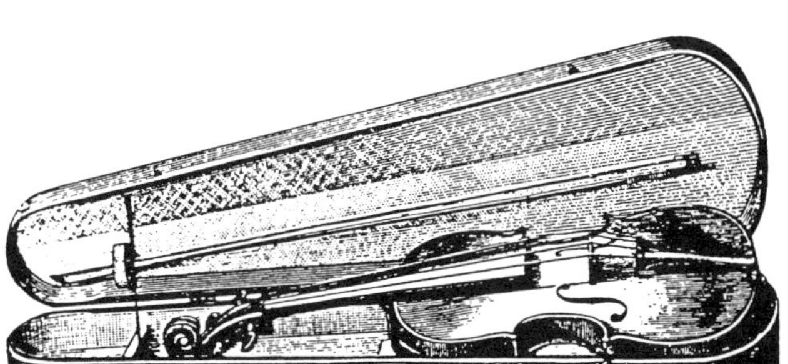

VESPER ROUND

Russian

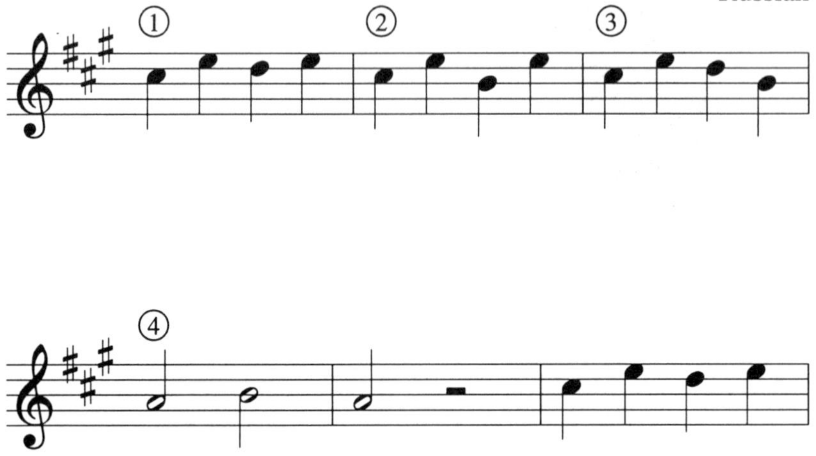

It is fun to play this 18-measure song as an 18-part round, making everyone a soloist!

VESPER – ORCHESTRA PART

SOPHOMORE LEVEL REPERTOIRE

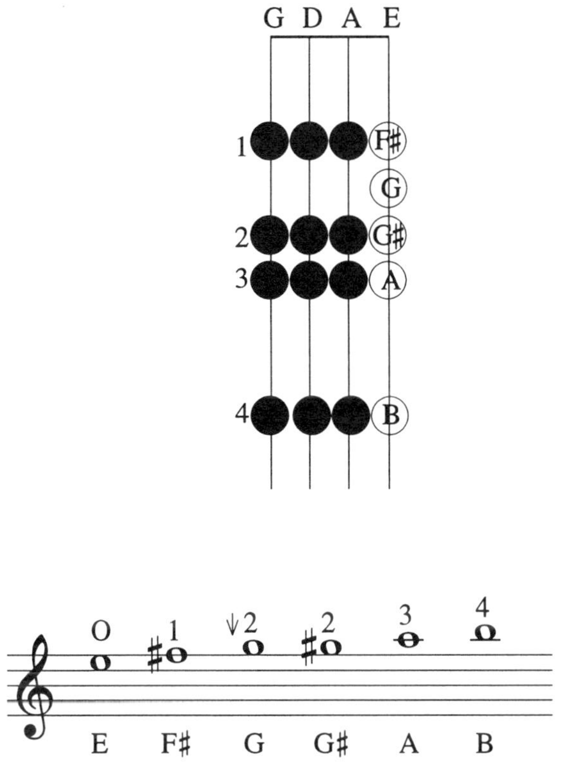
G D A E
1 F♯
G
2 G♯
3 A
4 B
0 1 ↓2 2 3 4
E F♯ G G♯ A B

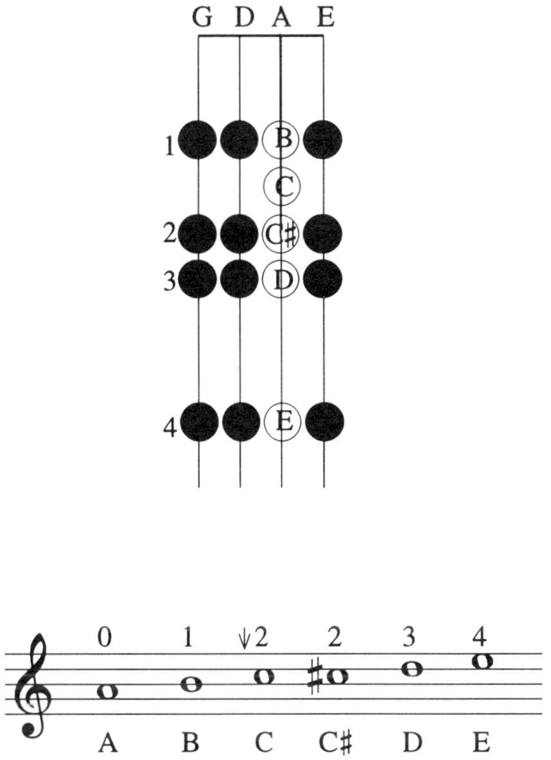
G D A E
1 B
C
2 C♯
3 D
4 E
0 1 ↓2 2 3 4
A B C C♯ D E

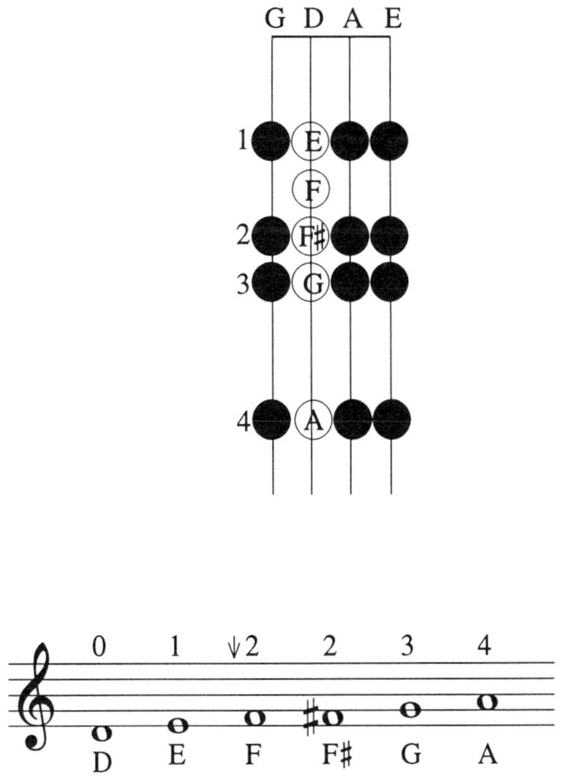
G D A E
1 E
F
2 F♯
3 G
4 A
0 1 ↓2 2 3 4
D E F F♯ G A

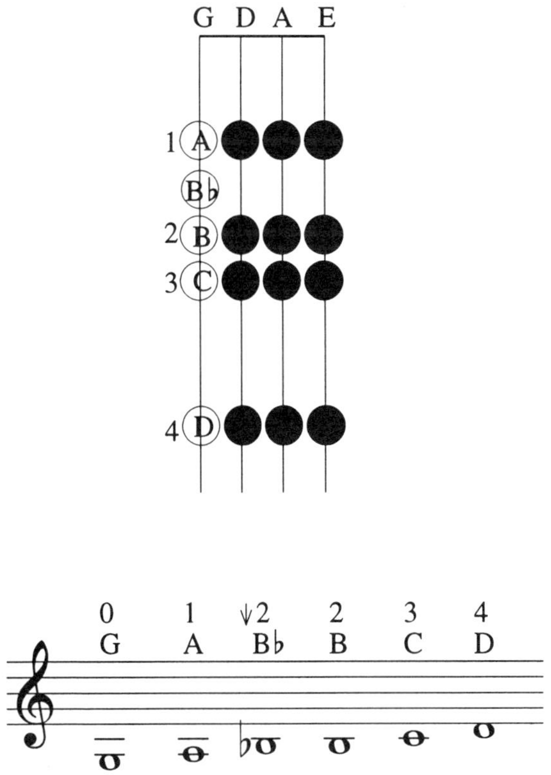
G D A E
1 A
B♭
2 B
3 C
4 D
0 1 ↓2 2 3 4
G A B♭ B C D

COME AGAIN, HO

English

OH MUSIC, SWEET MUSIC

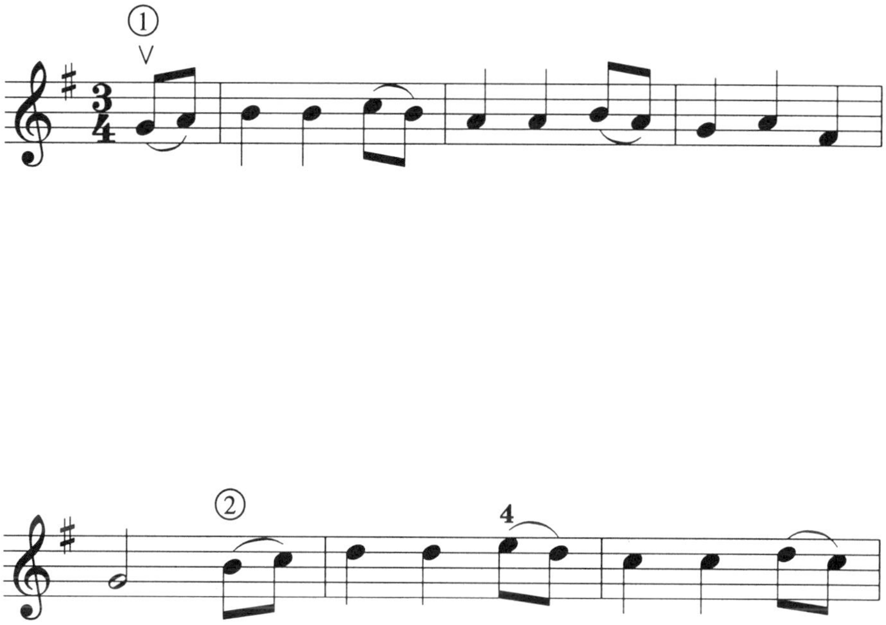

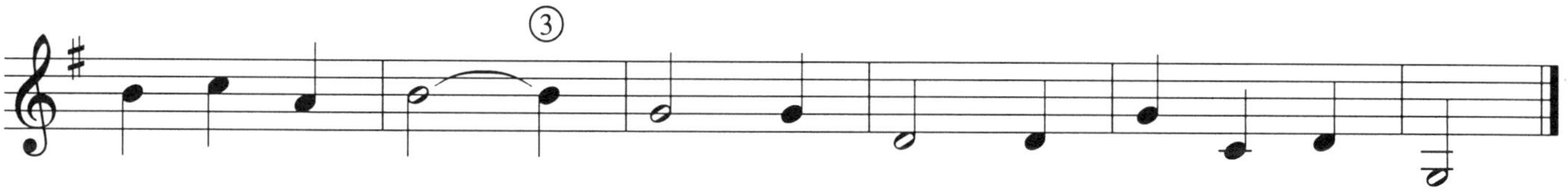

HEY NONNY NO

English

PEACE AND PLENTY

GOOD HOSTESS

The fermata sign indicates the end of the piece for each voice.

THE INVISIBLE FOX

John Hilton

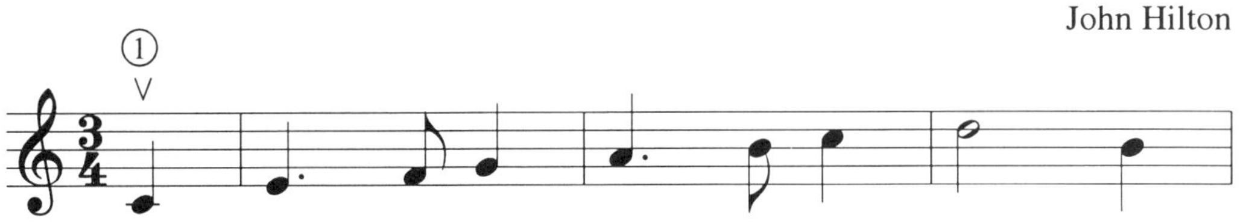

THE JOLLY HUNTER

①

②

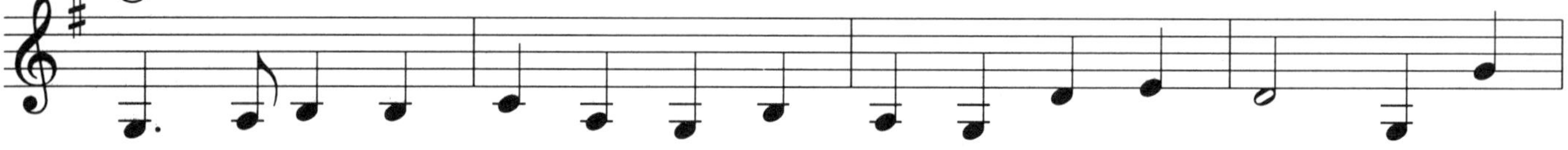

③

④

SI CANTEMO

Caldara

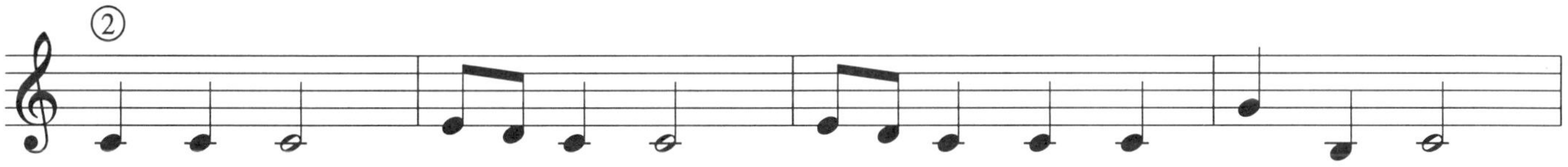

THE SINGING SCHOOL

SHALOM CHAVERIM

Israel

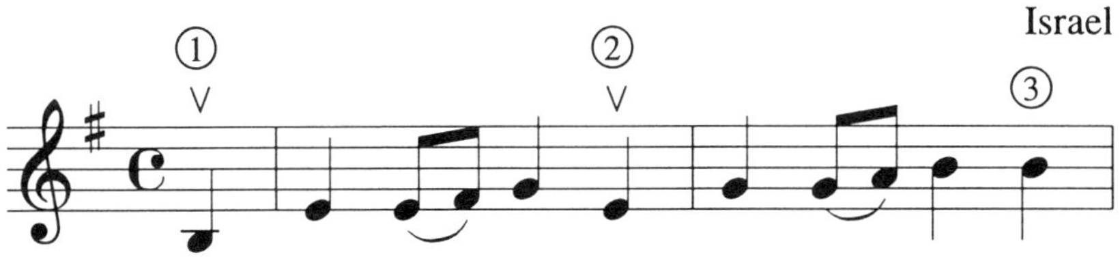

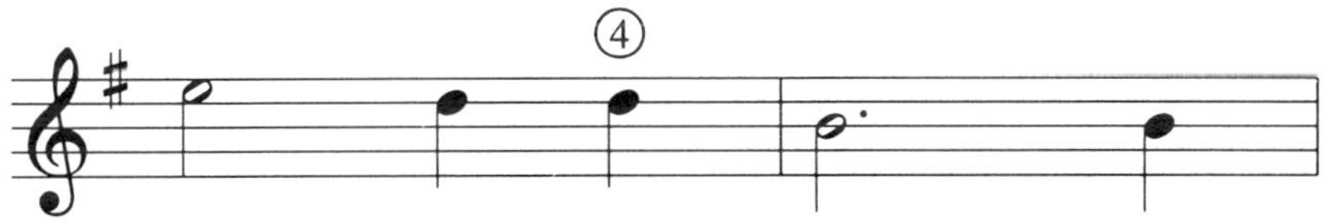

THE MIGHTY TOM

Henry Aldrich

ECHO YODEL CANON

Austrian
St. Aegyd.
Osterreigh 1894

For violins alone.

ORCHESTRA

Austrian

REVEILLE

(Bugle Call)

A MERRY HEART

Wm Lawes

DONA NOBIS PACEM
(Give Us Peace)

Palestrina

ROUND IN G MAJOR

Henry Purcell

JUNIOR LEVEL
REPERTOIRE

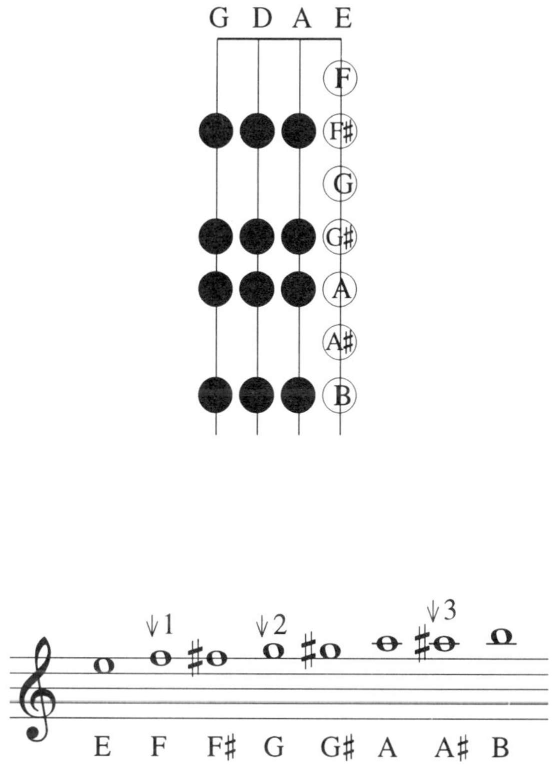
G D A E
F
F♯
G
G♯
A
A♯
B
↓1 ↓2 ↓3
E F F♯ G G♯ A A♯ B

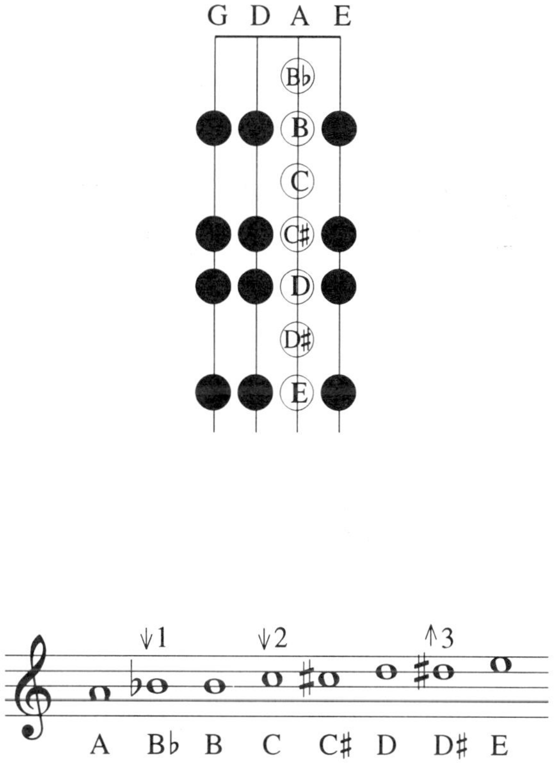
G D A E
B♭
B
C
C♯
D
D♯
E
↓1 ↓2 ↑3
A B♭ B C C♯ D D♯ E

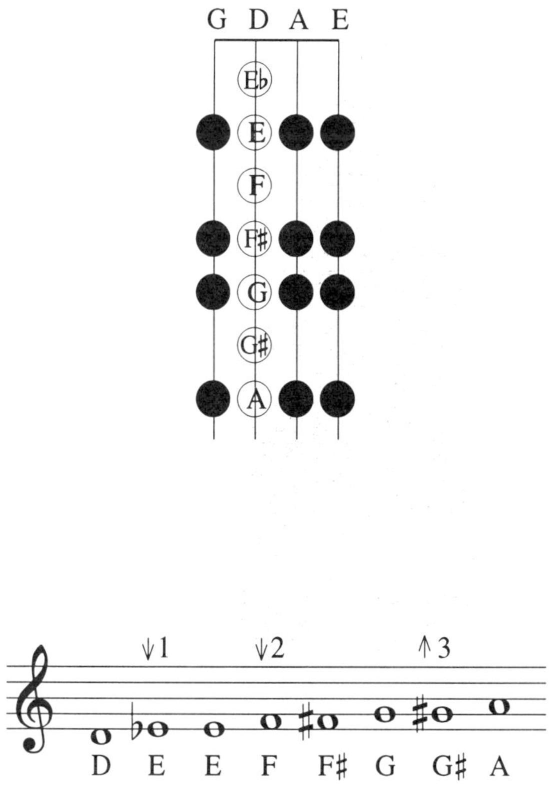
G D A E
E♭
E
F
F♯
G
G♯
A
↓1 ↓2 ↑3
D E♭ E F F♯ G G♯ A

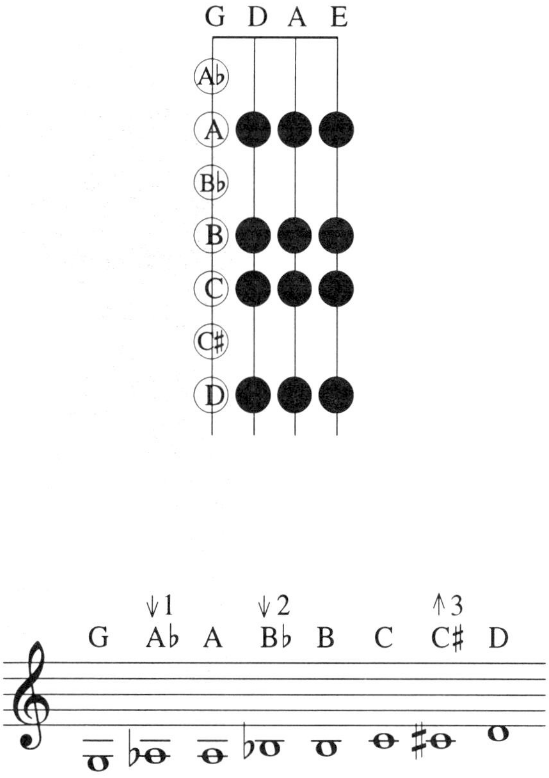
G D A E
A♭
A
B♭
B
C
C♯
D
↓1 ↓2 ↑3
G A♭ A B♭ B C C♯ D

ROSE

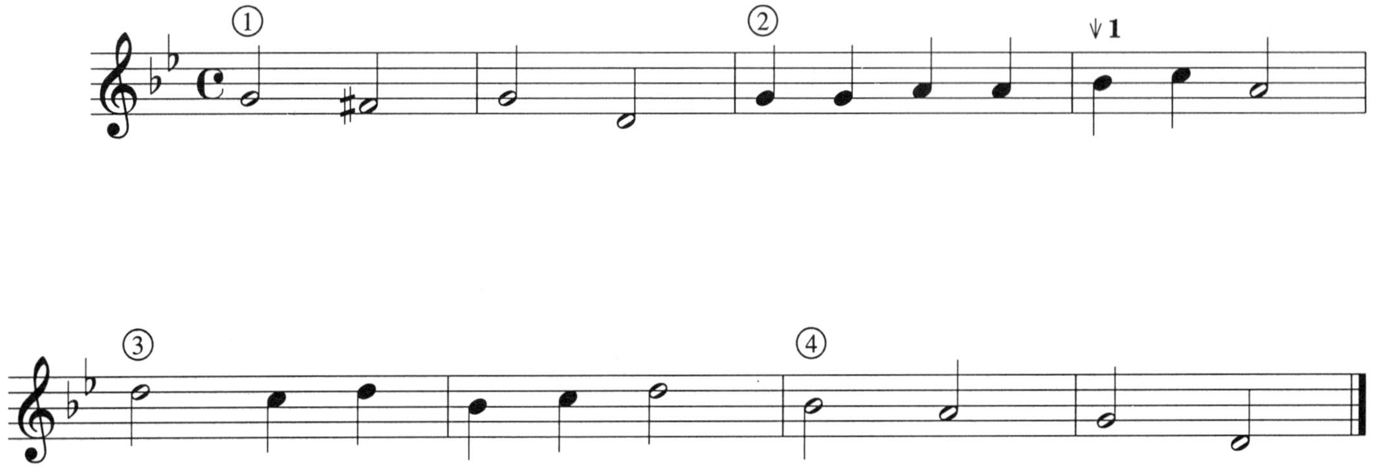

JUST TEASING

French

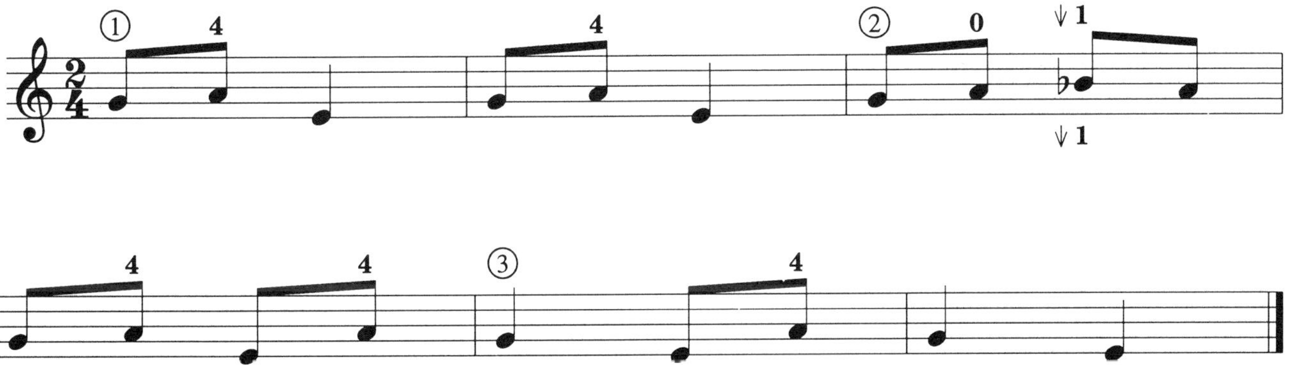

HEIGH HO, ANYBODY HOME

English

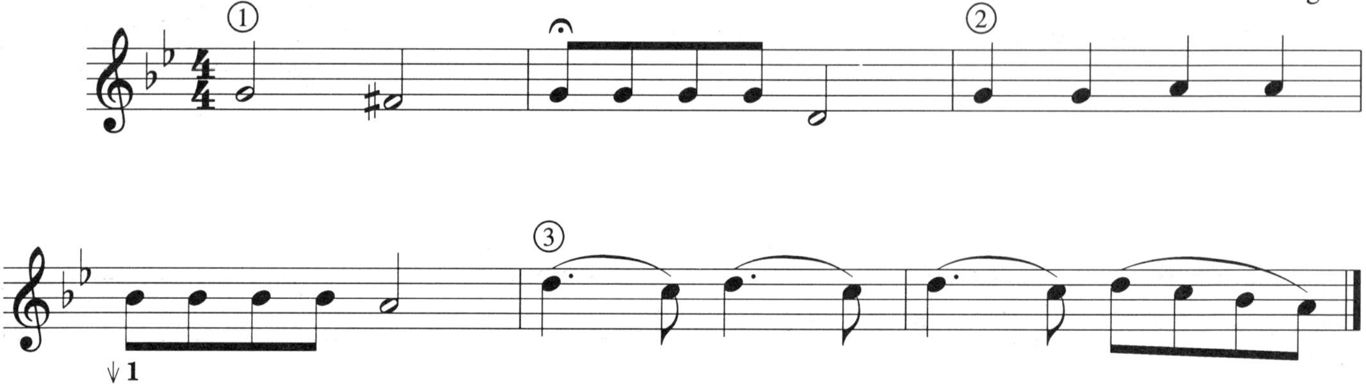

LET US SING TOGETHER

Czechoslavakian

SLEEP, BABY, SLEEP

Brahms

The fermata sign indicates the end of the piece for each part.

Brahms

THE ORIOLE CANON

Dutch

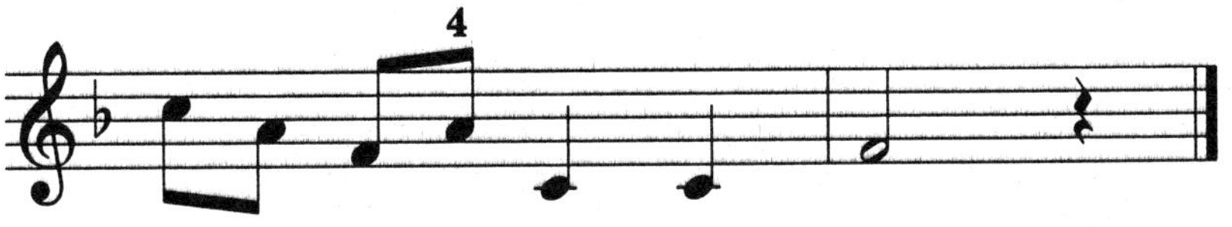

For violins alone.

WHO'LL BUY MY ROSES

A Quodlibet of Three
Foreign Folk Songs

②
③

FAIR URSLEY

G. Berg

THE HUNTERS

SUMER IS ICUMEN IN

English

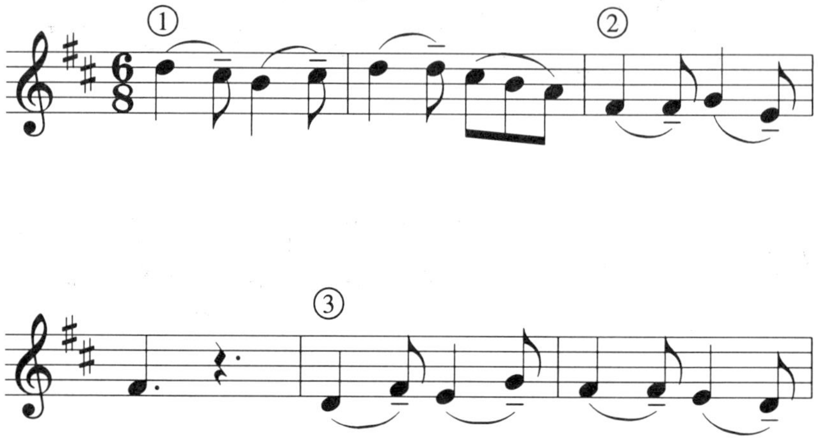

ALL WHO SING

Goodbar of Canterbury

LIFE SPAN

Purcell

THE STREET CRIES OF OXFORD TOWN

English

OAK

Hayes

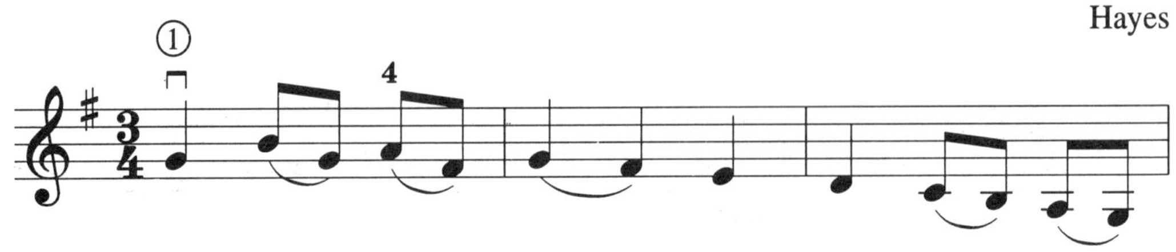

THE SWEET PLEASURES OF SPRING

BEETHOVEN'S ROUND

BARCAROLLE

19th Century

Accompaniment

SENIOR LEVEL REPERTOIRE

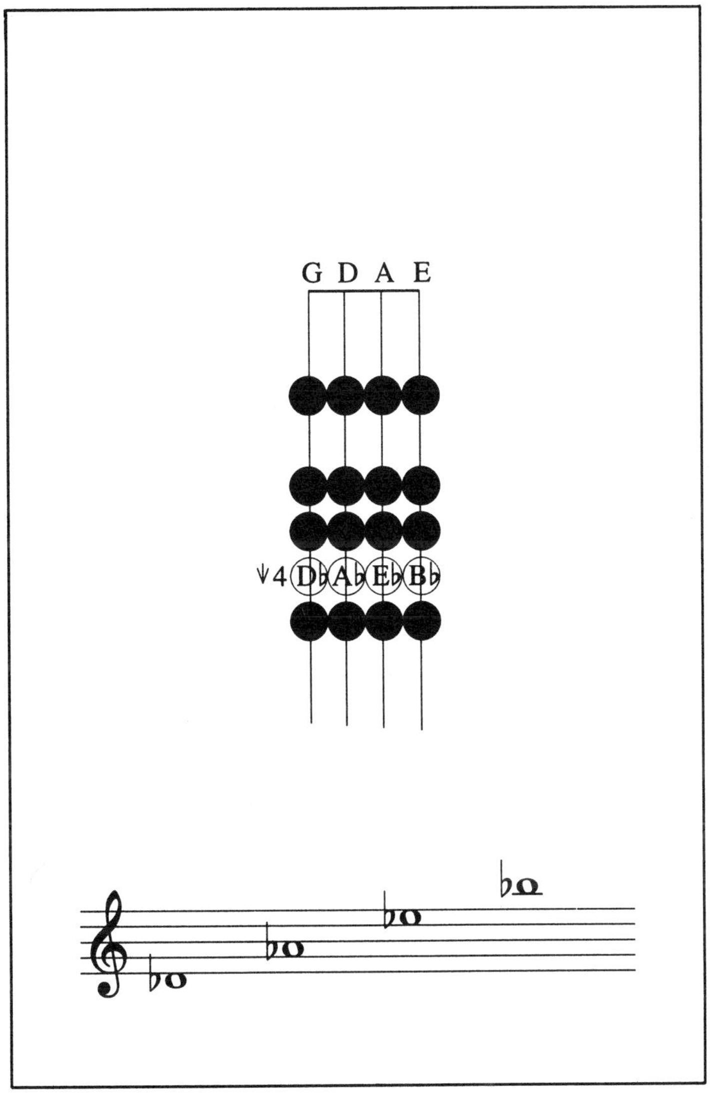
G D A E
4 D♭ A♭ E♭ B♭

PRATTY NAUN

John Hilton

SING AND BE MERRY

George Berg

SING WE THIS ROUNDELAY

English

AVE MARIA

Gregorian Chant

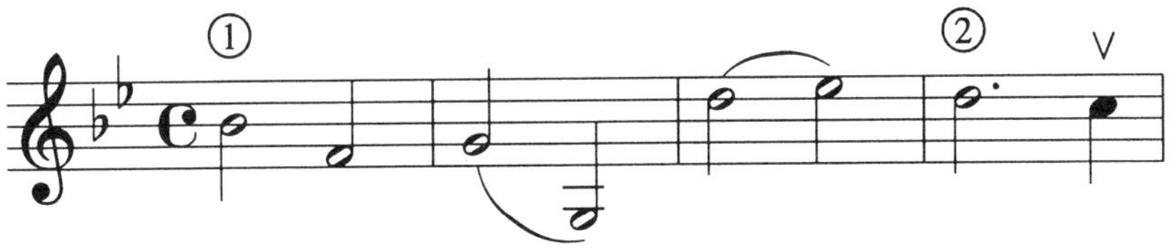

BONONCINI'S SPRING

GABRIAL JOHN

Purcell

CALLCOTT'S ROUND

NOW WE ARE MET

Samuel Webber

COME HITHER

John Hilton

THIS HOUR, MY BONNY LADS

Wm. Cranford 1652

ONE, TWO, THREE

Henry Purcell

TREAD SOFT MY FRIEND

Danby

RETREAT

Bugle Call

TO THE COLORS

Bugle Call

HAIDA, HAIDA

Jewish
East Europe

Presto

AS WE MINGLE OUR VOICES, WE MINGLE OUR SOULS

Henry Purcell

PACHELBEL'S KANON

13
14
15
16
17
18
19
20
tr
21
22
23

24
25
26
tr
27
28
29
tr
30
31
32

33
34
35
36
37
38

39
40
41

Piano accompaniment

Pachelbel

20
24
28
32
37